THE T-WALLS of KUWAIT and IRAQ

PALISADES PARK PUBLIC LIBRARY
257 SECOND STREET
PALISADES PARK, NJ 07650

EDITOR'S NOTE:

This book was created as an historical document and as a means to help the wounded from the conflict in the Middle East. My late father, Captain (Dr.) Emanuel Hauer, a Surgeon with the 3rd Field Hospital, U.S. Army, won the Bronze Star for saving fourteen GI's who had been shot or stabbed in the chest during the invasion of Luzon, Philippine Islands, 1945. He told me in later years that those soldiers suffered life altering injuries so my life would be secure, and that if a wounded soldier needed help, one should give it without being asked.

The net proceeds from this book will provide a portion of care to the wounded. Those brave men and women should never be forgotten. They have given too much. This book and effort to help the wounded are a tribute to my father's memory.

George Hauer

Text by Robin Whitney, Dedication by Chaplain (Col.) Craig N. Wiley, Artist's Forward by Warren Kimble, Graphic Design by Alan C. Ellis, Editor George Hauer

---

ACKNOWLEDGEMENTS

The publishers wish to acknowledge the assistance, advice and encouragement of the following:
David T. Robertson and Thomas Loikith of Harwood Lloyd, LLC, Hackensack, NJ for their assistance and advice on legal matters related to this project, Frank Duffin of Wiggin and Dana, LLP New Haven, CT for assistance on copyright matters. Sarah F. White, former Deputy Assistant Secretary of the Army, James Ball, Col. (Dr.) Gerard P. Curran, Col. Stephen P. Jones, LTC Michael, S. Davis, LTC Norman C. Fox, Major Anthony F. Beatman, Jeffrey T. Smith, Dr. Donald Rankin USAF (Ret), CIT-Services, LLC, Don Allen, Ethel Anne Chorney, Joseph FireCrow, Larry Kalbfeld, Daria Novak, Amaar Al-Hayder, Michael Paolini, CPA, Donald Peters, and Jose 'Tony' Vega.

DEDICATION

This beautiful book is dedicated to the thousands of American Service Members and Coalition Partner Nations who have braved the battlefields of Kuwait and Iraq to fight against the enemies of freedom.

It's been said that a picture is worth a thousand words. Within the pages of this book you will see how cement structures, intended for barriers, are transformed into pictorial walls that identify military units and honor service members who gave their lives for freedom. They provide an Esprit de Corps for their unit members who are forward deployed from their home base, post, or camp. The unit colors and insignias displayed on these walls become the thoughts and memories of the men and women who have fought, and for those who have died for freedom.

Some of these artistic wall paintings were created by Service Members of our Coalition Partner Nations. Throughout the War on Terror they have fought and died alongside their American partners. We pay tribute to them and give thanks for their sacrifice.

You will see memorial walls that proclaim in silence, the ultimate sacrifice of serving one's country. We must never forget the sacrifice that war brings.

These painted walls represent Soldiers, Sailors, Airmen, Marines, Coast Guard and D.O.D. Civilians who answered the call of freedom and deployed far from home and family. When these walls decay and are turned to rubble, this book will become a lasting legacy to those who have served in Kuwait and Iraq.

Today, thousands of military members of our Armed Forces are battling the tragic wounds of war, both mental and physical. The net proceeds from this book will go 100% to a multitude of charities that work with our wounded warriors and their families.

Lastly, let us give thanks to those whose vision it was to compile these pictures and make this fantastic book a reality. Your selfless service does not go un-noticed.

Chaplain (Colonel) Craig N. Wiley
United States Army

Forward From An Artist's Perspective

I was pleased and honored to be asked by George Hauer, a fellow alumnus of Syracuse University Class of 1960, to help select the artistic images for this book about the murals on the T-Walls of compounds in Kuwait and Iraq.

The art is the purest of folk art. Soldiers working as individuals, or as a team, created these creative depictions of every day war that are so impermanent. Soldiers, men and women artists, may be untrained, have a relative who influenced them, a school art class, or were professional artists before arriving in a war zone. The well established logos of a unit, show a fine sense of design and use of color and execution. In observing these artists' work note the excellence of design in the choice of lettering that evokes and enhances the spirit, strength and power of each wall.

Art is seeing and reproducing one's experiences. These paintings depict visual perceptions of their past and present situations. I wonder how the experience of designing and painting these murals will affect their present and future creative works. Art surrounds us all our lives no matter who we are or where we are. These warriors are expressing what is going on in their present environment through art.

Warren Kimble
Contemporary folk art represented in many private and public collections worldwide
BFA Syracuse University, 1957
Honorary Dr. of Fine Arts, Green Mountain College
In the collection of Shelburne, Museum, Shelburne, VT
George Arents Pioneer Medal. Syracuse University Outstanding Alumni Award

Units Included

(Some National Guard units appear in this section.)

Pages 10 through 149

ALAMO (THE)-JAG OFFICES CAMP ADDER

ANACONDA POWER AND LIGHT
(Power plant at Joint Base Balad)

ARMY TRANSPORTATION CORPS

Balad Association of Doctors

Anaconda Surgical Society

BANDIT PRIDE

CATFISH AIR-Helicopter passenger
terminal, Joint Base Balad

DEFENDER (THE)

FRA STRYKER/CAMP ANACONDA

G-FSC

JOINT BASE BALAD

LBA- ANACONDA LAW ENFORCEMENT

LVIS

MISSISSIPPI RIFLES

MORTARITAVILLE (USO)

MORTY'S GARAGE-BALAD

MOUNTAIN RANGERS

MRAP

NAVAL CUSTOMS DELTA CO.

NAVY PETROLEUM DETACHMENT

NPDB-5

PHIPPS TROOP CLINIC

Pittsburgh Steelers Terrible Towel

PT/OT JOINT BASE BALAD

RED CROSS

SEABEES 7+12 NMCB

SOLDIERS CREED

TASK FORCE JAYHAWK

TASK FORCE KEYSTONE

TASK FORCE SABER

TASK FORCE 26

TASK FORCE 34 COMBAT AVIATION
BRIGADE

TASK FORCE118 MMB

TASK FORCE 163

TUSKEGEE AIRMEN

TUSKEGEE MEDICS

VETERANS DAY

VIKING WARRIOR

1/17 ARTILLERY

1-18TH INFANTRY

1-35 ARMOR (BAUMHOLDER, GERMANY)

152ND AVN

1-85TH AVIATION

1-100TH AVN

1-110TH INFANTRY

1-114TH INFANTRY

1-126 AVN REG. MEDEVAC

1-130TH ATTACK

1-131ST AIR BRIGADE

1-131ST ARMOR

1-137TH AHB

1-137TH E CO.

1-150TH AHB

1-151 LOGISTICS AVIATION

1-155TH INFANTRY/D CO.

1-159 AIRBORNE

1-161ST INFANTRY

1/179TH DELTA CO.

1/179TH 45TH INFANTRY/E CO.
(OKLAHOMA)

186TH MP CO.

1-189TH AVN

1-200TH A & C CO.

1-244TH AVN

1-293RD INFANTRY

1ST ARMORED-4TH BRIGADE

1ST CAVALRY DIVISION

10TH CO. SUPPORT HOSPITAL
(FT. CARSON, CO)

10TH SBTB

11TH SIGNAL BRIGADE

16TH SUSTAINMENT BRIGADE

101ST ENGINEERS

102ND QM CORPS.

104TH MP BATTALION

106TH TC & 13TH CSSB/213TH

111TH POSTAL COMPANY
120TH FSC (HOBART, OK)
121ST BSB
122ND SUPPORT CORPS (SELMA, AL)
123RD MOBILE PUBLIC AFFAIRS DET.
126TH AVN-1ST BATTALION
130TH ENGINEER BN
130TH SIGNAL BN
133RD MEDICAL DET. (HANAU, GERMANY)
137TH AVN
138TH FIRE BRIGADE
142ND ENGINEERS
151 AVN
153RD MP CO.
162ND INFANTRY-HHC2
164TH SUPPORT GROUP
166TH REGIONAL SUPPORT GROUP
172ND INFANTRY
175TH INFANTRY
178TH MILITARY POLICE
182ND SAPPER
185TH AVN
188TH AVN
186TH ENG. CO. (DOTHAN, AL)
186TH SUPPORT CO. CSE
193RD AVN
194TH ENGINEERS
196TH TRANSPORTATION CO.
2ND TRANSPORTATION CO.
(FT. RICHARDSON, AK)
2-10TH AVN
2-104TH GSAB
2-104TH AVN
2-114 AVN

2-127TH INFANTRY BATTALION
2-149TH AVN B CO.
2-149TH AVN DELTA CO.
2-149TH CSAB
25TH COMBAT AVIATION BRIGADE
27TH BSB ALPHA CO.
28TH MED A & B
28TH CAB
29TH BSB
29TH FIELD ARTILLERY-3RD BATTALION
203RD MP CO.
209TH AREA SUPPORT BATTALION
213TH AREA SUPPORT
215TH ASMC
220TH MP CO.
223RD MEDICAL DETACHMENT
245TH AVIATION REG. TF SOONER
248TH ASMC MEDICS
259TH COMBAT AVIATION BRIGADE
259TH CSSB
277TH ASB
287TH SUSTAINMENT BRIGADE
296TH TRANSPORT CO.
3-6TH FIELD ARTILLERY
3-82ND FIELD ARTILLERY
3-158TH
3-297TH ASB
3-509TH
3RD ARMORED CAVALRY DIVISION
3RD CORPS SUPPORT COMMAND
30TH ENGINEERING BRIGADE
30TH SIGNAL BATTALION
31ST INFANTRY REGIMENT
34TH CAB

35TH SIGNAL BRIGADE
35TH SIGNAL BATTALION
36TH HHC
36TH SUSTAINMENT BRIGADE
37TH AIRBORNE SAPPER
37TH FINANCE
301ST ASG
304TH CHAPLAIN
304TH MP BN
304TH SUSTAINMENT BRIGADE
307TH MEDICAL CO.
314TH CSSB
325TH CSH
326TH ASG
332ND AIR EXPEDITIONARY WING
332ND ECES
332nd EFES
332ND ESFS
332ND EFCS
332ND EMDG
332ND VEHICLE MAINTENANCE
332ND TRANS. FLIGHT GROUP
345TH CSH
350TH HRC
351ST CSBN
354 MPAD
366TH AIRBORNE
377TH TRANSPORTERS
382ND FIELD ARTILLERY
3666 SMC
4-25TH RANGERS
4-27TH ARTILLERY
4-123RD AVN B CO.
4-159TH AVN REGIMENT

4TH BRIGADE ARMORED
4TH ENGINEERS
4TH SIGNAL BATTALION
40TH CORPS SUPPORT GROUP
40TH EXPED. SIGNAL BATTALION
40TH MP
44TH MEDICAL CO.
45TH AIRBORNE
45TH INF-1-179TH
45TH SUSTAINMENT BRIGADE
6TH EXPEDITIONARY SIGNAL BATTALION
402ND FIELD SUPPORT BRIGADE
415TH AVN REGIMENT
425TH AVIATION REG. 1ST BATTALION
425TH CABN
444TH AIRBORNE
463RD ENGINEER BATTALION
464TH MEDICAL CO.
5-509 RANGERS
55TH MEDICAL CO.
56TH INFANTRY-(FT. BRAGG)
56TH STRYKER
507TH CORP SUPPORT GROUP
510TH SAPPER ENGINEERS
536TH MAINTAINANCE CO.
(SCHOFIELD, HAWAII)

541ST PERSONNEL
546TH MAINTAINANCE CO.
551 MED CO (FT. LEWIS, WA)
557TH ERHS
557TH MED CO.
563RD SUPPORT AVIATION-A CO.
582ND MEDICAL LOGISTICS
64TH MEDICAL DETACHMENT (V.M.)
603 MP CO.
607TH MP BN
628TH ASB
639TH CS CO.
7TH CAVALRY-5TH SQUADRON
7TH MPBN
7TH SIGNAL BRIGADE
(MANHEIM, GERMANY)
7TH SUSTAINMENT BRIGADE
7-158TH AVN
72ND EXPEDITIONARY SIGNAL BATTALION
(MANHEIM, GERMANY)
76TH INFANTRY BRIGADE
716TH MILITARY POLICE
732ND AIR EXPEDITIONARY GROUP
732ND ECES
732ND ESCS
732ND ESFS

732ND INTEL. SQUAD
732ND MCT USAF
732ND MEDICAL MCT
735TH MSB A CO.
744TH MP CO.
769TH BATTALION ENGINEERS
770TH AIRBORNE
8TH CAVALRY
8TH MP BRIGADE
80TH ORD. BN (JACKSON, TN)
81ST MMT
89TH TRANSPORTATION CO.
810TH MILITARY POLICE
826TH ORD. CO.
834TH ASB
840TH DEPLOYMENT & DISTRIBUTION
864TH ASRB
887TH ESFS
9TH ENGINEER BN-B CO.
9TH SUPPORT BN-B CO.
90TH SUSTAINMENT BRIGADE
910 QM
957TH MRBC
1123RD TRANSPORTATION CO.
1387 QM (GREENVILLE, MISSISSIPPI)

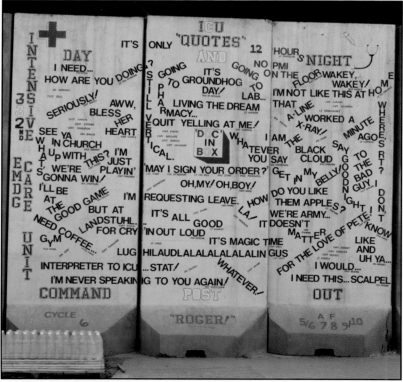

"For much of the last six years, as a soldier arrives or departs Iraq, his first or last stop is a camp in Kuwait. Dependent on the time of year, you are usually hit in the face by a breeze that feels like a hair dryer, or hot coals near your face at a barbecue. In the summer it is commonly 125-130 degrees Fahrenheit. This is real hot, like below zero is real cold. The next thing that is clearly different from home is how the desert is huge and flat. It reminds me of what I imagine the ocean floor would look like, without the water. While Iraq has more varied terrain, and even trees, Kuwait is strikingly stark. After the terrain and weather, the next striking thing about Kuwait is the large number of T-walls. T-walls are steel reinforced concrete molded barriers that are usually ten to fifteen feet tall and eight to ten feet wide. They were introduced into Iraq and Kuwait in the late 2004-2005 time period as blast protection against the common, poorly aimed, rockets and mortars in Iraq. Soldiers in that period typically lived in sand bag protected tents, which were quite vulnerable to these threats. T-walls provided real protection against the horizontal ripping shrapnel and concussive blast of a near miss to the areas where we lived, worked and slept."

June 2010
Gerard P. Curran, Commander, COL, MC
118th MMB – Multifunctional Medical Battalion
Connecticut Army National Guard

With his first hand description, Colonel Curran gives us our first powerful introduction to the context of the murals photographed for this book.

Wikipedia, the on-line encyclopedia, has an informative entry describing these industrial constructions, which are called "Bremer walls" here. According to this source, "A Bremer wall is a twelve-foot high (3.7 m) portable, steel-reinforced concrete wall of the type used for blast protection, throughout Iraq and Afghanistan. The name is believed to have originated from L. Paul Bremer of the Coalition Provisional Authority, who was the Director of Reconstruction and Humanitarian Assistance for post-war Iraq following the Iraq War of 2003 in the early years of the Iraq War.

The Bremer barrier resembles the smaller 3-foot (1m) tall Jersey barrier, which is used widely for vehicle traffic control on coalition military bases in Iraq and Afghanistan. To indicate that the Bremer barrier is similar but larger, the 12-foot (3.7 m) tall intermediate-sized Bremer

barriers are usually referred to as Texas barriers (but not to be confused with the 3½ foot (1.1 m) Texas constant slope barrier) By this same naming convention, the largest barriers, which stand around 6 meters (20 ft) tall, are called Alaska Barriers. Unlike the Jersey barrier which has sloped-sides at the base, the Texas and Alaska barriers have a rectangular ledge (usable as a bench for sitting or resting) which is approximately knee high for a typical adult. Alaska barriers are typically used as perimeter fortifications of well-established bases in Iraq and Afghanistan.

These T-shaped walls were originally developed by the Israelis in the Israeli West Bank barrier. The term "T-wall" is commonly used by soldiers throughout Iraq and Afghanistan, due to their cross-sectional shape resembling an inverted letter T."

On a purely experiential level these elaborate T-walls must surely shock. The photographs collected in this book challenge us to imagine this immense desert with endless flat terrain and its truly monumental scale nearly bleached of color. In this exotic landscape the impact of the sudden intrusion of thousands of bright, endlessly imaginative images must surely astound. Through these photographs we

can begin to experience the cacophony, action, colors and the endless and astonishing variety of activities that these vibrant images thrust upon the enormous, largely silent and nearly featureless landscape that surrounds many of the military installations.

James Ball, Assistant Red Cross Station Manager, who took many of the photographs in this book, writes the following to describe his experience at Joint Base Balad in Iraq, "I want to emphasize that the T-Wall cannot be taken out of the context of a war zone with incoming mortar and rocket attacks weekly, loud and impressive F-16 jets taking off at all hours of the day and night, camaraderie at the base cafeterias, standing at attention at the beginning of every movie shown at the Base theater for the playing of the national anthem, and not least the helicopters coming in with wounded soldiers

Integrity First

732ⁿᵈ MCT
USAF

Service Before Self

ELRS
132D EXPEDITIONARY LOGISTICS READINESS SQUADRON
COMBAT AIRMEN

1Lt K. McDowell	SMSgt J. Criger
TSgt M. Williams	TSgt E. Cruz Jr.
SSgt J. Clouatre	SSgt S. Christian
SSgt W. Engle	SSgt O. Polina
SrA R. Gaeth	SrA J. Kliewer
SrA A. Laski	SrA D. Steward
A1C T. Akau	A1C N. Cocchiarella
A1C O. Sanchez	A1C A. Wilkinson

Excellence in All We Do

WE NEVER STOP

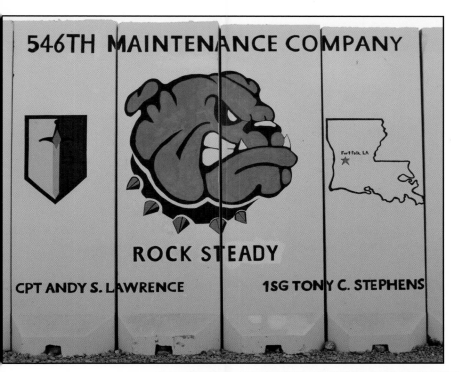

546TH MAINTENANCE COMPANY

ROCK STEADY

CPT ANDY S. LAWRENCE   1SG TONY C. STEPHENS

to the base hospital. It is all one mosaic with T-walls representing one impressive part of the puzzle." He describes many thousands of people living and working on this giant military installation. The population consists of thousands of military personnel from all branches of the U.S and coalition armed forces, many of them women. The base also houses thousands of non-military private contractors and additional thousands of citizens from the developing world, many of whom do not speak English and are hired to clean,

REGULATORS

LONG KNIFE

4

EX ANIMO

ALPHA COMPANY 27th BSB 1CD

CPT MONTGOMERY   1SG GRAHAM

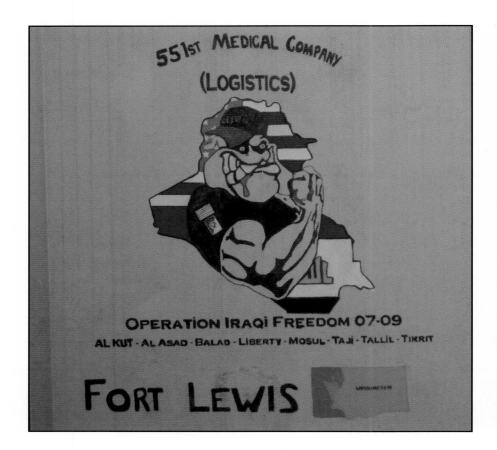

cook and do most of the unskilled work of the base. He describes the Ugandan soldiers who guard the entrance to the main dining hall and the Nepalese man who does not speak English but who cleans the Red Cross office on the base. He described the swimming pools and the many entertainments of the base such as sports contests and holiday celebrations. The large base is a place consisting largely of containerized housing and workspaces made up of shipping container like structures. These are all surrounded by and interspersed with thousands of sections of steel reinforced concrete blast walls, known as T-walls, many of which are twelve to fifteen feet high and many sections wide. It is these many acres of impersonal

Readiness Power, *Forward*

and blank concrete walls that the soldiers saw fit to fill with images and artwork and which were used in such imaginative ways to personalize and transform their environment.

The general public, of course, is not the intended viewer of these works. The soldiers created these works by themselves and for themselves. They did not intend to communicate with anyone other than themselves and each other. But the images they chose, the subjects they chose, the fantasies they celebrate and the memories they honor are powerful messages which speak to universal, timeless human impulses: identify with your particular group, make your surroundings distinctively your own, reference your experience, your culture and your time in this particular place and space. Many of the walls serve as memorials for fallen comrades and carry a powerful charge of grief and loss and memory for some of the military units.

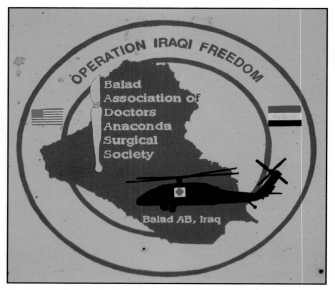

As outsiders, how many different ways can we approach these images to grasp the fullest possible impact of their meaning? Of course, soldiers and wayfarers from time immemorial have left their mark on the landscapes through which they passed. "Kilroy was here," and so was the Spanish explorer-soldier Juan de Oñate who carved his name and the date into a stone canyon wall in New Mexico when his expedition passed by on "16 of April 1605." On the most elementary level the decorated blast walls serve a similar purpose, to document in some way the presence

and the experience of the unusual combination of people and purpose that came together at this place. The steel reinforced concrete T-wall sections were designed for blast protection, rapid assembly and transport. They serve a very necessary and vital purpose: to provide safety and protection to those behind it. Of course, the secure nature of these structures also demands that they serve to isolate inhabitants from the street and each other. The blank walls demand uniformity and lack distinguishing characteristics. With every wall identical to the next, unadorned, they would serve to disorient and to confuse. The actions of the soldier-artists powerfully overcome the disorientation and the uniformity inherent in a maze of anonymous cement walls. In the hands of the artists the walls become distinctive, memorable and meaningful through the art placed on them. The artwork powerfully erases any sense of anonymity, isolation and disorientation. The paintings on the T-walls proudly announce and identify each unit, serve as powerful memorials or celebrate and inspire. They make each sector unique

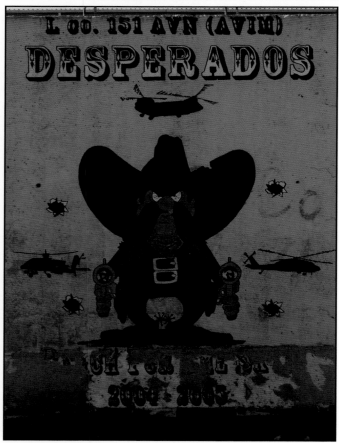

and memorable and bridge the gulf of isolation caused by the nearly impenetrable barrier of the wall itself. Many of the walls tell us, and whoever passes by, useful and necessary information: who is where. The mechanics are here, the Kansas National Guard is there, the military police are around the corner. In this regard the works are strictly utilitarian and necessary and provide information in a compelling way. The common element in much of this monumental wall art is in the purpose and the intention to identify which group is located where. These "identification tags" in the early days of an American presence in these places were rather simple and straightforward nametags. Quickly they evolved into something much more complex and meaningful. They continue to identify the group in residence but, in addition, become a way to celebrate and to honor these groups, their histories, their origins and their cultures. We find familiar local American icons taking up residence far from home. The

Kansas Jayhawk, and the familiar Native American warrior image, are both endowed with new meaning and significance. Again and again we see the art honoring the history and tradition of the past while it strives for new understandings, new expressions and new symbols of inspiration and honor. We see memorial walls too, and those which honor commanding officers and unit heraldry.

How is it that these artworks speak to us on so many levels? Looking at these works carries an immediate jolt of emotion and fascination, recognition and intrigue that compel us to analyze our strong reactions and to try to understand why our response is so immediate and so compelling. Americans, of course, will bring to their experience of these works a strong sense of the current events which inform the works and their personal connections to the events and the people involved: the war in Iraq and the American soldiers, direct participants in this history.

These artworks serve to change our perspective from watching history unfold on our television screens to a more ground level appreciation of the location, the atmosphere and the soldiers' impact on and interaction with their environment. Through these monumental murals we somehow gain a sense that history and current events are happening around us and even through us on a level far more personal and immediate than we ever assumed or imagined. These works may jolt us or surprise us or intrigue us but through them there is no doubt that our perspective shifts and our minds and hearts are jolted into a more direct and visceral relationship to the soldiers and the events. Through these works we are honored to be invited to share some of the soldiers' most personal thoughts and feelings, their instincts, their priorities, some of their sense of their own identity, and their sense of their place in history and indeed in time. We are honored by the opportunity to experience their values, their creativity, their inspiration, and to come to see what these extraordinary soldiers honor, what they memorialize

and what they celebrate on a very personal and somehow even intimate level. We can appreciate the sense of humor and lament the losses. We can find here a sense of triumph and pride as well as a sense of unrelenting loss and sacrifice.

The images on the T-walls thrust an astonishing variety of emotions and images and information upon the very fabric of the built environment. Here at home, the one or two favorite wall murals in any city can become favorite icons of place. It is an entirely different concept for the murals to be nearly contiguous and to be themselves the defining feature of both street and building. The murals seem somehow stunningly American while at the same time, like all great art, speak to common human themes and experiences. The environment they create when experienced as a monumental group, must be somehow truly new and daunting.

A DEFENDER IS
SOMEONE WHO
STEPS UP
WHEN
EVERYONE
ELSE BACKS
DOWN

CPT OVERTON

582nd MedDog

SECOND TO NONE

Log Dawgs

1LT COTTON   CW2 BATISTA

BALAD

AL ASAD   LIBERTY   MOSUL

TIKRIT   TALLIL   TAJI

If the city is considered a living organism, then we must surely recognize that with these military installations the city has evolved to a new level of meaning and experience. From a culture of billboards, advertising, commerce, and popular culture, the soldiers have taken the techniques, the impact and the scale and have achieved a truly powerful re-imagining of the American tradition of promotion and entertainment. They have used familiar materials, and many times familiar images, monumental scale and attention grabbing graphic design techniques and have fundamentally transformed them in their use, their expression, their purpose and their meaning.

In addition, this art makes it clear that a new generation is on the scene. Contrast this art to that of our World War II soldiers. At that time pin-up girls seemed to dominate the subject matter and there was a strong sexual content to much of the work. Are military censors at work in Kuwait and Iraq or have the sensibilities of the soldiers changed this dramatically? Does the presence of so many female troops, a defining characteristic of 21st century U.S. military life, contribute to

the change in sensibility? In addition, the soldier art of the 1940's frequently taunted the enemy, and much of the art was placed on the exceedingly transitory structure of the airplanes or, indeed, the bombs themselves. As Colonel Curran writes, "T-walls are similar to the nose art of the bombers of World War II, but I think they are more complicated in their themes, mostly due to the larger area the artists have to express themselves, and the diversity of the artists. They are especially similar, in that they're perishable. These T-walls will eventually

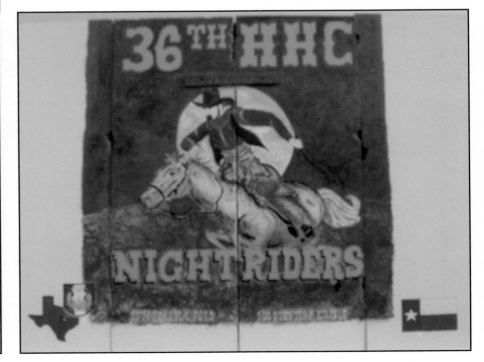

be ground into pebbles, or the art will literally be 'sand blasted' away by nature. This book of photos is an attempt to help convey their messages, and to allow our fellow Americans to see the art that expresses the feelings of common people facing a serious challenge on a personal and group level."

We may lament that these works cannot be a permanent mark on the landscape. They are created on multi-sectional cement blast walls that are designed to be transported and are easily disassembled. The T-walls are outdoor features covered with delicate paint and by force of circumstance required to endure one of the harshest climates on earth. They endure searing heat, bleaching, unrelenting sun and ferocious scouring sandstorms, not to mention the occasional rocket or mortar blast. They are transitory, and this adds to their power. Like life itself, the seasons, and both war and peace, the works don't merely tell us about the transitory nature of human reality,

but are themselves a powerful visual example of one moment in human history, as they inevitably fade, bleach, chip, and are slowly or quickly eroded or dismantled. Their presence in a remote, dangerous location also adds to their power since few will experience them directly but can only know them through photographs. This isolation, of course, in itself dilutes their reach and modulates their meaning. Perhaps we should be grateful for this inevitable distance and separation. We recognize that few of us could withstand the actual experiences and living conditions common to these warriors, the climate

and the battle, the separation from loved ones, which grieves them, and the fierce bonding brotherhoods, which sustain them. History and experience require a new imagining of time and place and these artworks are powerful proof that a new time and a new place have indeed come into existence, at least for these uncommon men and women in a very exotic and forbidding place and circumstance. We are honored to be allowed a glimpse into their world through these photographs.

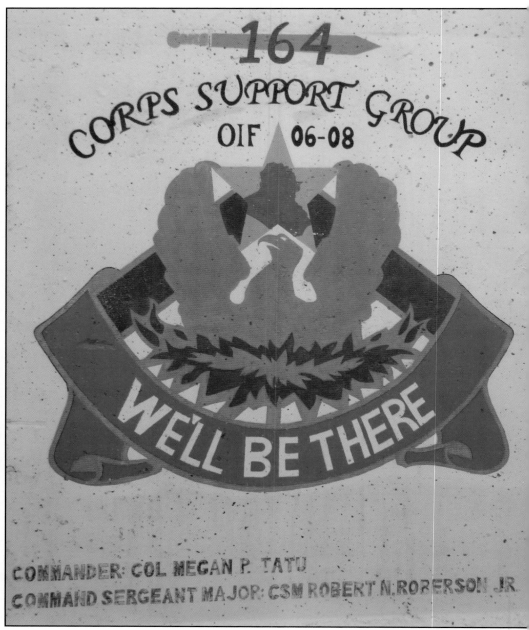

COL David W Fitzgerald
CSM Edward Ramsdell

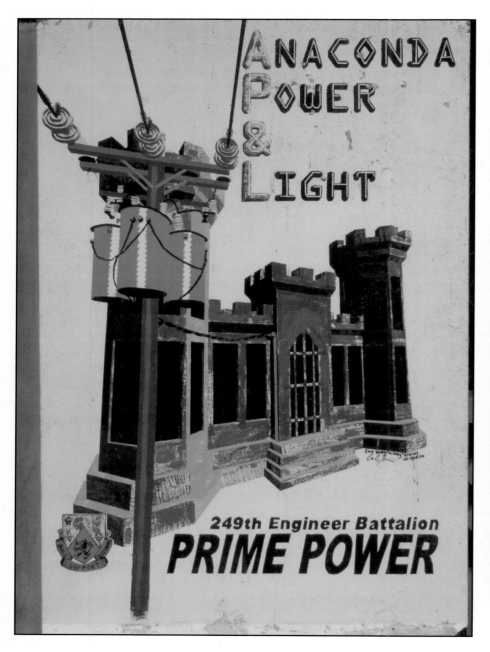

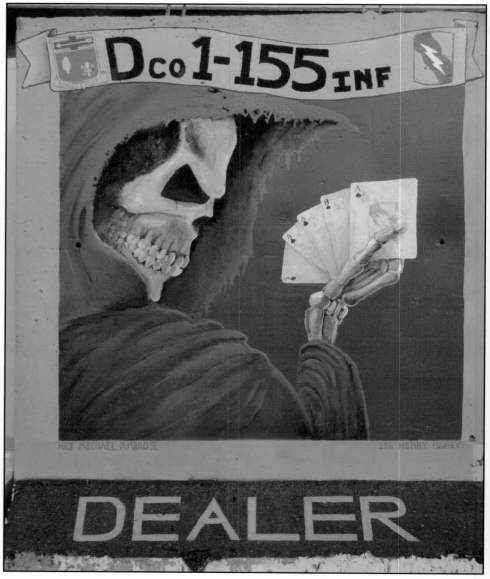

507th Corps Support Group (Airborne)

Let's Roll

40th Corps Support Group

DRAGONSLAYERS

OIF IV

COL Jannett N. Jackson
Commanding

CSM Michael E. Baker
Command Sergeant Major

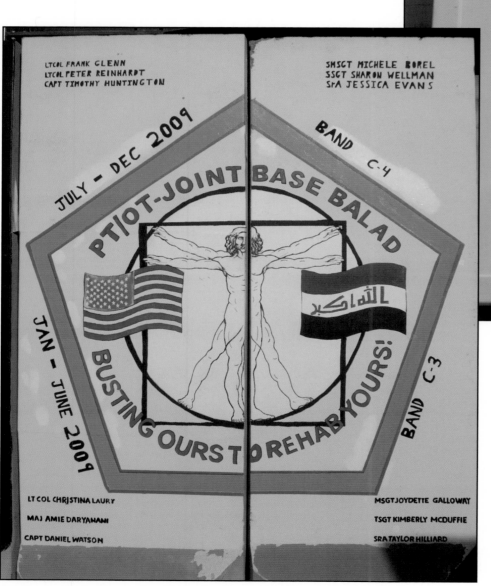

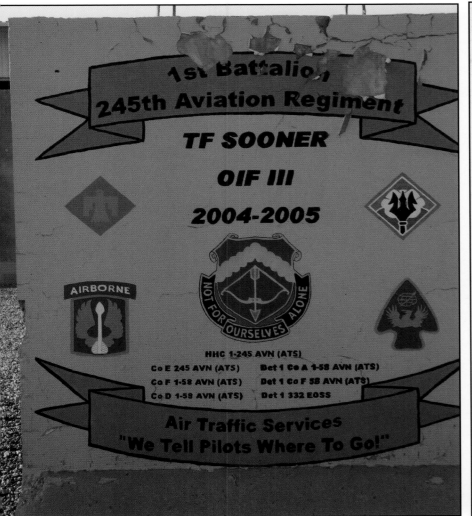

1st Battalion
245th Aviation Regiment

TF SOONER

OIF III

2004-2005

NOT FOR OURSELVES ALONE

AIRBORNE

HHC 1-245 AVN (ATS)
Co E 245 AVN (ATS)   Det 1 Co A 1-58 AVN (ATS)
Co F 1-58 AVN (ATS)   Det 1 Co F 58 AVN (ATS)
Co D 1-58 AVN (ATS)   Det 1 332 EOSS

Air Traffic Services
"We Tell Pilots Where To Go!"

4TH BRIGADE 1ST ARMORED DIVISION

1

HIGHLANDER

STRENGTH AND HONOR

13

IT SHALL BE DONE

UNITY IS STRENGTH

INSISTE FIRMITER

FIDELIS ET VERUS

UTTMOST IN HONORABLE SERVICE

STEADFAST LOYAL TRUE

COL PETER A. NEWELL

CSM PHILLIP D. PANDY

MILITARY SURFACE DEPLOYMENT AND DISTRIBUTION COMMAND

840TH DEPLOYMENT AND DISTRIBUTION SUPPORT BATTALION

VANGUARDS

TASK FORCE

IN OMNIA PARATUS

OIF 06-08

1-18TH INFANTRY

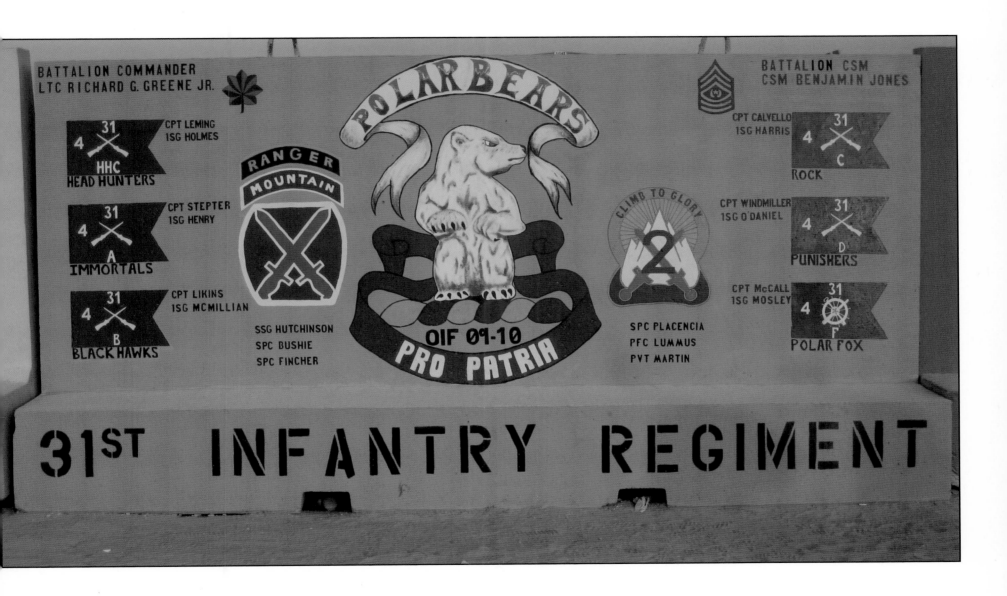

BATTALION COMMANDER
LTC RICHARD G. GREENE JR.

BATTALION CSM
CSM BENJAMIN JONES

CPT LEMING
1SG HOLMES

4 31
HHC
HEAD HUNTERS

CPT STEPTER
1SG HENRY

4 31
A
IMMORTALS

CPT LIKINS
1SG MCMILLIAN

4 31
B
BLACK HAWKS

RANGER
MOUNTAIN

SSG HUTCHINSON
SPC BUSHIE
SPC FINCHER

POLAR BEARS

OIF 09-10
PRO PATRIA

CLIMB TO GLORY
2

SPC PLACENCIA
PFC LUMMUS
PVT MARTIN

CPT CALVELLO
1SG HARRIS

4 31
C
ROCK

CPT WINDMILLER
1SG O'DANIEL

4 31
D
PUNISHERS

CPT McCALL
1SG MOSLEY

4 31
F
POLAR FOX

31ST INFANTRY REGIMENT

5th Squadron 7th Cavalry

Apache

Bandit

Combat

TF Warpaint

Dealer

HeadHunter

Rock

ONLY THE DEAD HAVE SEEN THE END OF WAR ~ PLATO

OIF '07 ~ '08

366th

444th

LIBERTY

479th

HHC

FSC

770th

C/864th

AIRBORNE

LT. COL.
WALTER

CSM.
DOBRANSKI

SAPPERS

123rd **Mobile Public Affairs Det.**
Operation Iraqi Freedom 08-10

CPT Jeffrey A. Johnson
1LT Holly C. Moody
1LT Ray K. Ragan
MSG Max D. Hamlin
SSG Tonya R. Gonzales
SSG Aaron C. Thacker
SGT Alexander L. Gago
SGT Lorne W. Neff
SGT Crystal G. Reidy
SGT Alexander N. Snyder
SGT Monette A. Wesolek
SPC Mario A. Aguirre
SPC Brian A. Barbour
SPC Kelly A. Beck
SPC Roger L. Bemis
SPC Charles J. Bohm
SGT Tom W. Bramble
SPC Kiyoshi C. Freeman
SPC Jacob R. Smathers

MAJ Christopher A. Emmons
Commander

1SG Reginald M. Smith
First Sergeant

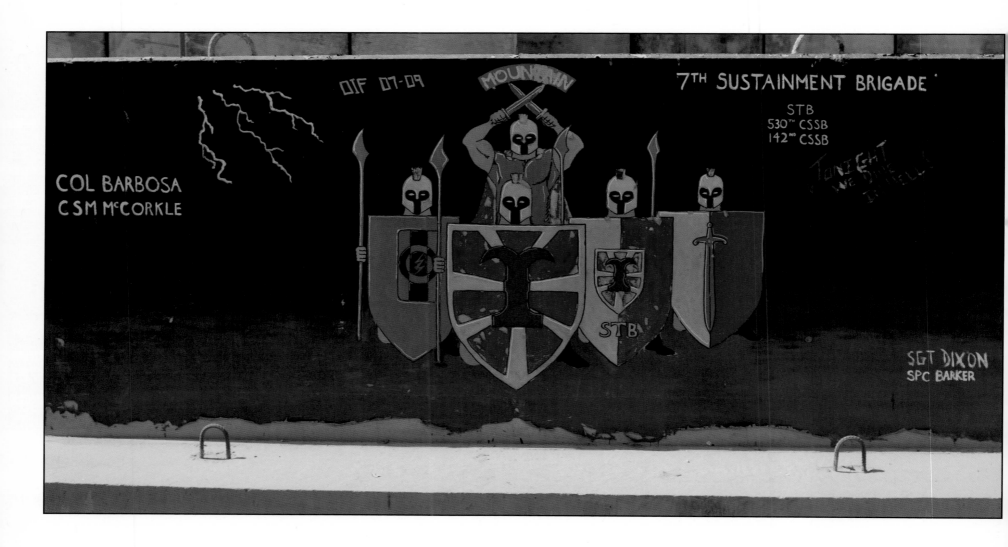

325th Combat Support Hospital

COMMANDER: COL HAILE
CSM: CONKLIN

TO FIGHT FOR LIFE

WARRIOR·MEDICS·TRAINED
>READY<

>OIF<
07-08

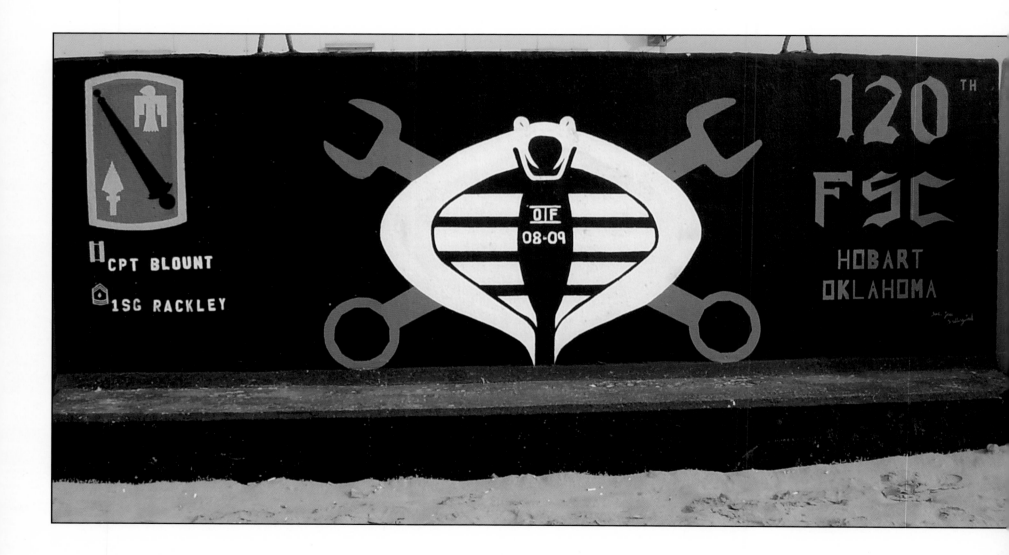

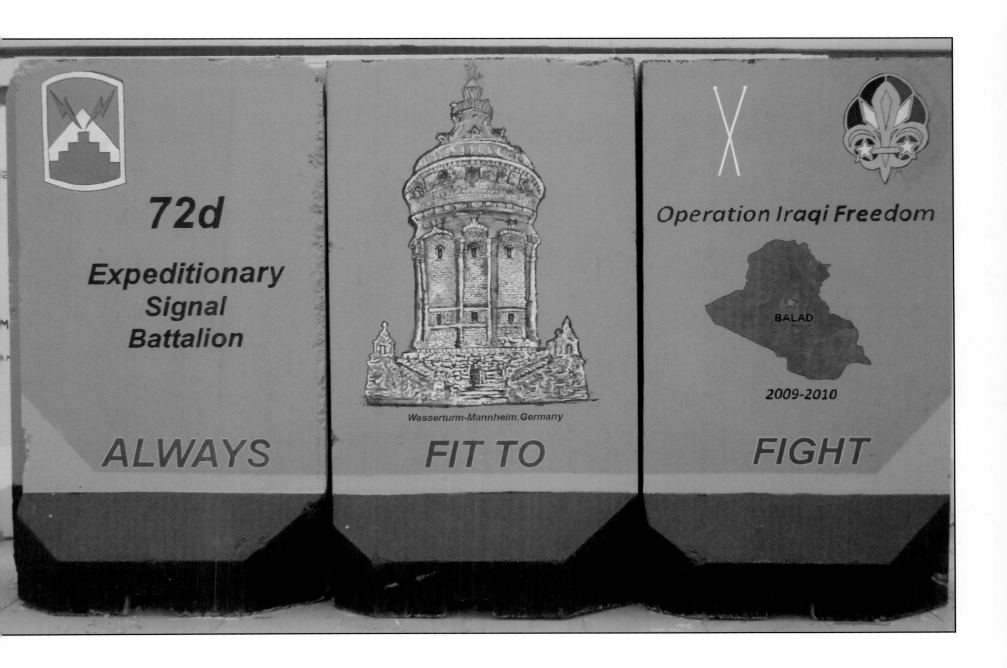

72d

**Expeditionary
Signal
Battalion**

Wasserturm-Mannheim, Germany

Operation Iraqi Freedom

BALAD

2009-2010

ALWAYS

FIT TO

FIGHT

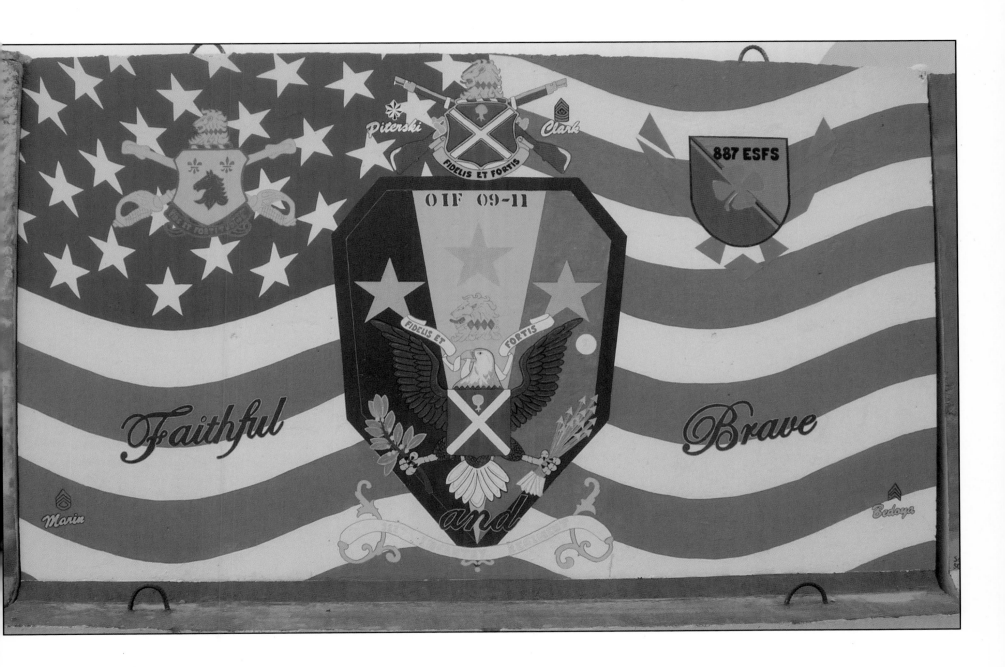

Faithful *and* Brave

OIF 09-11

887 ESFS

FIDELIS ET FORTIS

716TH MILITARY POLICE BATTALION

THE MOST DECORATED MP BATTALION IN THE WORLD

AIRBORNE

HHD

1SG Smith
CPT Brookshire

IRAQ
2007 - 2009

Painted by
Doc Powell

WORLD WAR I - VIETNAM

KOSOVO - AFGHANISTAN

PFC
Delaroche

PFC
BRANDON

PFC
CHRIS

CPT B
...

510TH SAPPER COMPANY

CONDITE ET PUGNATE

1SG John M.F. Etter   CPT Kenneth P. Rockwell

121st BSB
4th BCT
1st AD

LTC
WILSON

OIF 09-10

UTMOST IN HONORABLE SERVICE

CSM
MUSTAFA

IRON HAMMER

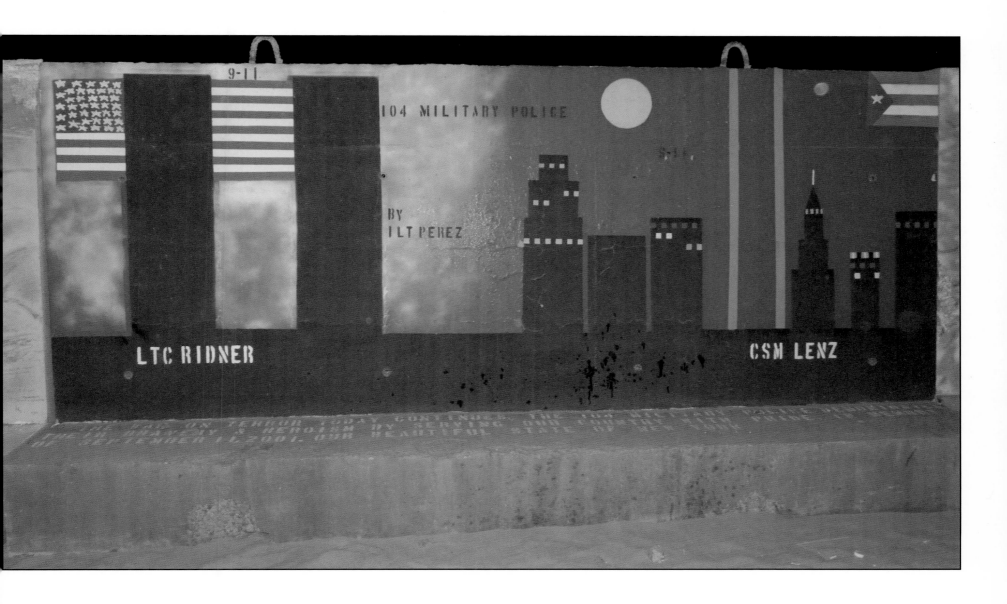

OIF 09-11

25TH COMBAT AVIATION BRIGADE

AVN

"WINGS OF LIGHTNING"

COL MIKE LUNDY
WINGS 06

CSM JESUS RUIZ
WINGS 07

GUNSLINGER – LIGHTNING HORSE – DIAMOND HEAD – HAMMERHEAD - LOBO

56TH INFANTRY BRIGADE COMBAT TEAM

THE

COL LEE HENRY

CSM JOHN M. MORGAN III

TIP OF THE SPEAR

OIF 09-11

ASSUME NOTHING - LEAVE NO DOUBT

LTC. SOLOMONS — CSM. STUCKEY

STALLIONS

EMDG
egee
Here,
110

Medics ...
Right Now
2006

5
5
7
To

THE

E
R
H
S
HORSE!

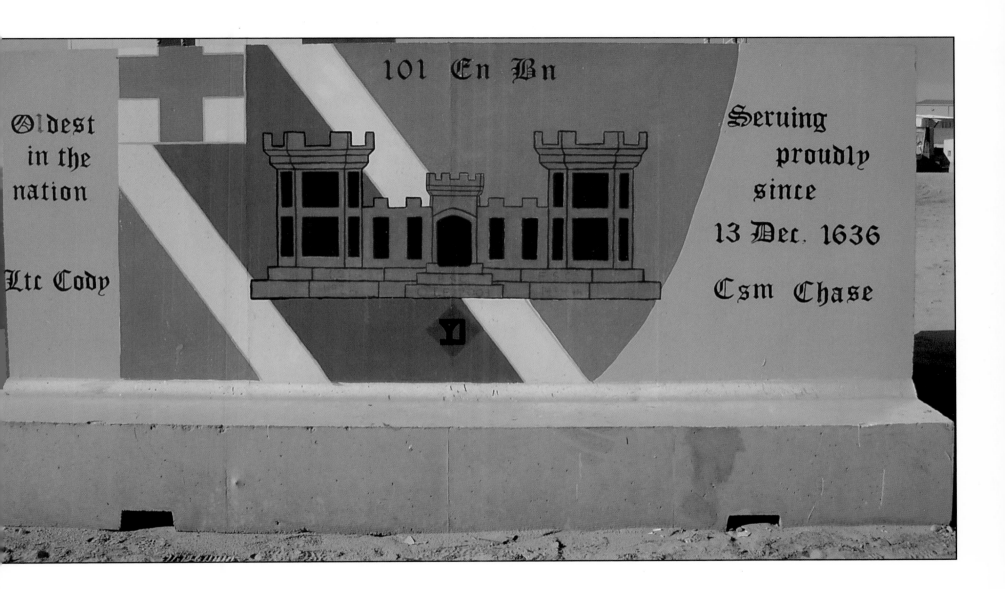

ANDERSON

GATOR BN
WISCONSIN

HELLHOUND
APPLETON

2-127

Strike Forward

OIF
09-10

BULLDOG
GREEN BAY

ZELLE

CHICKENHAWK
FOND DU LAC

2-127TH INFANTRY BATTALION

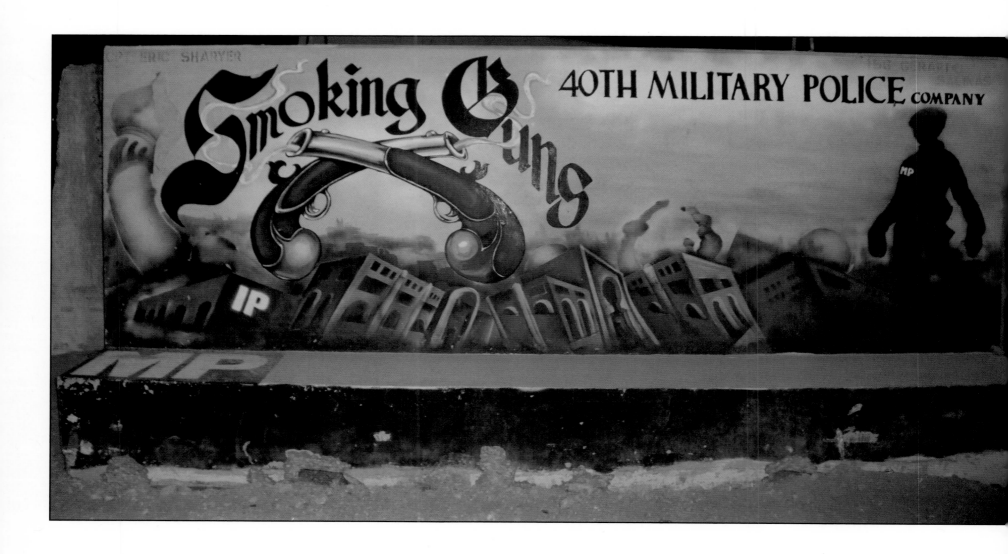

332 EMDG
Tuskegee Medics

Save Lives...
Clear the beds...
Take care of one another

The legend continues...

Right Care...

Right Here...

Right Now...

CPT. COLLITON   1SG LEVERY

RESPICIO TOTUS
VEREOR NULLUS

RESPECT ALL
FEAR NONE

1ST PLT 2LT ZIMMER   H CO 1-161 INF   OPS-MSG SKEAN
         SFC NOLTE   MEDICS-SGT FLETCHER
2ND PLT 1LT SCHOBER   SUPPLY-SGT BEACH
         SFC ROSS   MAINT-SSG MILLER
3RD PLT 1LT COCHRAN
         SSG ARNOLD   XO
                          1LT ALANIZ

Hustler

SGT Kouse
A H63 Det 3
Apache

TEAM G   TF 1-293 IN

1SG Ryan Bridgewater   1LT Christopher Stillions

Platoon Sergeants   FORT WAYNE   Platoon Leaders
   SSG Hess   1LT Hardy

   SFC Piercy   2LT Lich

   SFC Burge   1LT Yoder

GANGSTERS

9th En. Bn. B Co.

CPT. MAXA-CO.

1SG. FEILER   CPT. NGOUFAN X.O.

OUTLAWS

ROCKSTEADY!

O.I.F. 09-11

SCHWEINFURT, GERMANY

NATIONAL GUARD UNITS

ALABAMA	KANSAS	NEW YORK
ALASKA	KANSAS CITY, KANSAS	NORTH CAROLINA
ARIZONA	KENTUCKY	NORTH DAKOTA
ARKANSAS	MARYLAND	OKLAHOMA
CHICAGO	MICHIGAN	OHIO
CONNECTICUT	MINNESOTA	OREGON
COLORADO	MISSOURI	PENNSYLVANIA
DELAWARE	MISSISSIPPI	PUERTO RICO
HAWAII	NEW HAMPSHIRE	SOUTH CAROLINA
ILLINOIS	NEW JERSEY	TENNESSEE
INDIANA	NEW MEXICO	WASHINGTON
IOWA	NEW ORLEANS	WISCONSIN

RED TF 163 HAWKS

ARMS FOR SUPPORT

LTC VESPER
CSM KNIES

RAOC
CPT FIPPEN
1SG HOWER

A Co Berserkers
CPT HAYWOOD
1SG FULKERSON

B Co Mustangs
CPT MOTZ 1SG Weakley
HHSB 3-139 Desert Wolves
CPT PADGETT 1SG JENSEN

INDIANA NATIONAL GUARD

CW2 Bill Snook

153rd MP Co.

Delaware

CPT YAWN

1SG FIELDS

One Team One Mission

ALAMO DUSTOFF

FOR THE RIDE OF YOUR LIFE

OIF 08-10

TX   OK

C Co. 2-149 AVN

OKLAHOMA

MAJ Carlos Tamez

1SG Jon Polozeck

HERE I AM... SEND ME.   ISAIAH 6:8

203rd Military Police Battalion

ENFORCERS OF FREEDOM

LTC Charles Buxton
CSM Perry Hooper

OIF 09 – 11
Alabama Army National Guard

CPT Brad Priest
1SG Robert Larkin

CO. A 735TH MSB

MAINTAIN THE WHEEL

MISSOURI ARMY NATIONAL GUARD

4 JAN 2005   OIF III   20 DEC 2005

BG MYLES DEERING
45TH IBCT
COMMANDING GENERAL

LTC MARK PILKINGTON
1-179 INFANTRY
COMMANDER

LTC DOUG STALL
1-279 INFANTRY
COMMANDER

LTC DAVE JORDAN
1-160 FIELD ARTILLERY
COMMANDER

LTC DAVE JOHNSON
1-161 FIELD ARTILLERY
COMMANDER

CSM DEAN BRIDGES
45TH IBCT
COMMAND SERGEANT MAJOR

CSM JEFFRY MAPES
1-179 INFANTRY
COMMAND SERGEANT MAJOR

CSM KELVIN McHENRY
1-279 INFANTRY
COMMAND SERGEANT MAJOR

CSM LARRY DAVIS
1-160 FIELD ARTILLERY
COMMAND SERGEANT MAJOR

CSM HAROLD WHITLEY
1-161 FIELD ARTILLERY
COMMAND SERGEANT MAJOR

45TH IBCT

OKLAHOMA
KANSAS 2008 MARYLAND

SSG JOHN MATHEUS

Cpt. Grimaldi

1Sg. Kennebeck

186th MP Company

1st Plt. Ghostdawgs
2nd Plt. Wolfpack
3rd Plt. Rat Patrol

"PROUD AND READY"

IOWA

OIF

08-09

IOWA ARMY NATIONAL GUARD

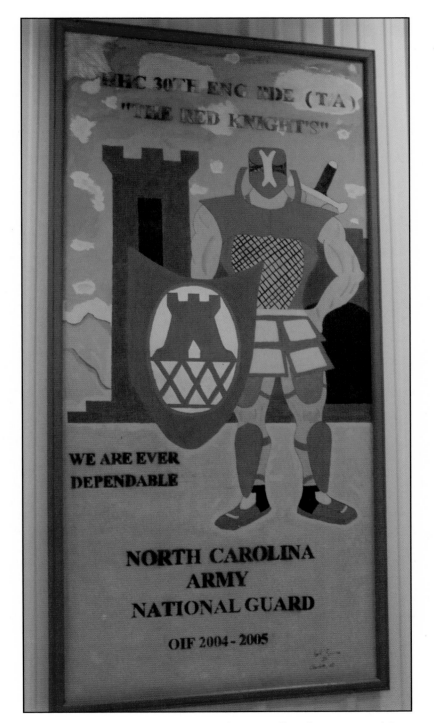

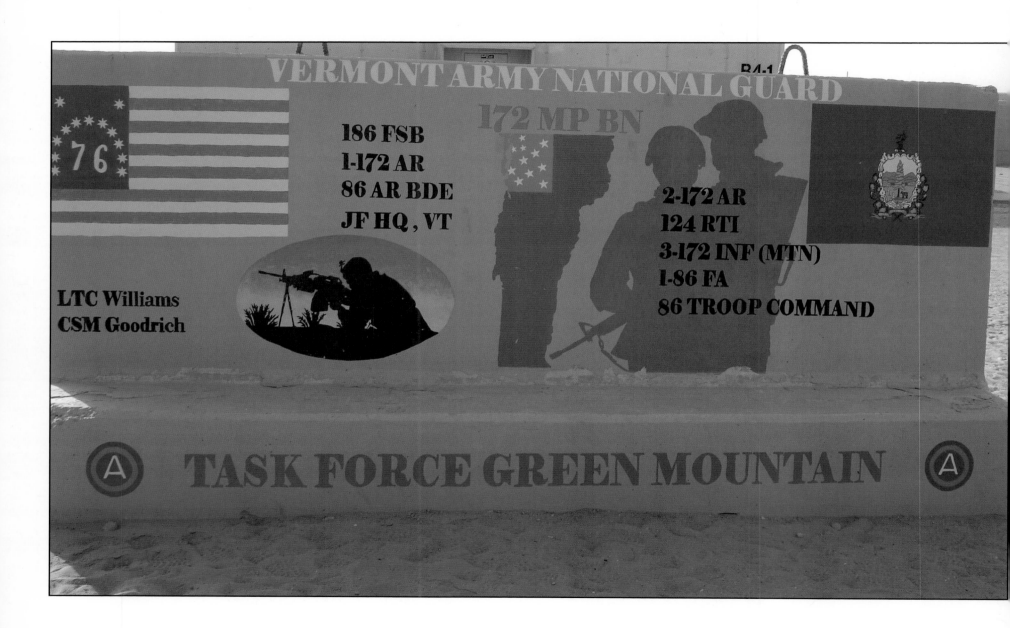

VERMONT ARMY NATIONAL GUARD

172 MP BN

186 FSB
1-172 AR
86 AR BDE
JF HQ , VT

2-172 AR
124 RTI
3-172 INF (MTN)
1-86 FA
86 TROOP COMMAND

LTC Williams
CSM Goodrich

TASK FORCE GREEN MOUNTAIN

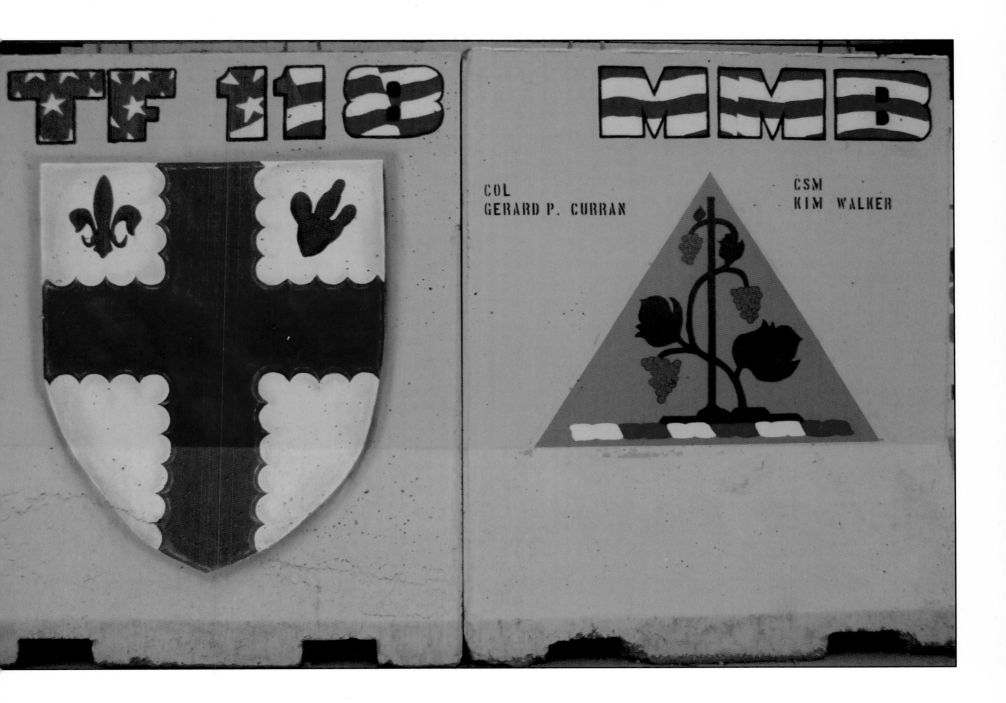

TF 118

MMB

COL
GERARD P. CURRAN

CSM
KIM WALKER

OIF
2008-09

287th Sustainment Brigade

"Sustain the Victor"

COL Robert F. Schmitt   CSM Timothy R. Newton

CPT Ed R. Bailey
1SG Thomas N. Sprague

HHC

287th Special Troops Battalion

"Warriors of the Plains"

LTC Tony D. Divish   CSM Manuel R. Rubio

SUSTAIN THE VICTOR

KANSAS

DK HELVIE

SGT M Albert

Killer Miller

194th ENGINEER BRIGADE

TENNESSEE ARMY NATIONAL GUARD

TASK FORCE
TITAN

BG ROBERT HARRIS
CSM CHARLES HUDSON

Washington Army National Guard
541st Personnel Services Detachment

Al Asad
Ar Ramadi
Baghdad
Kalsu

THE SEAL OF THE STATE OF WASHINGTON 1889

AIRBORNE

Tallil's First PSD
"It's All About You"

OIF 04-06

COALITION WALLS

AUSTRALIA

CZECH REPUBLIC

FRANCE

ITALY

NEW ZEALAND

ROMANIA

UNITED KINGDOM

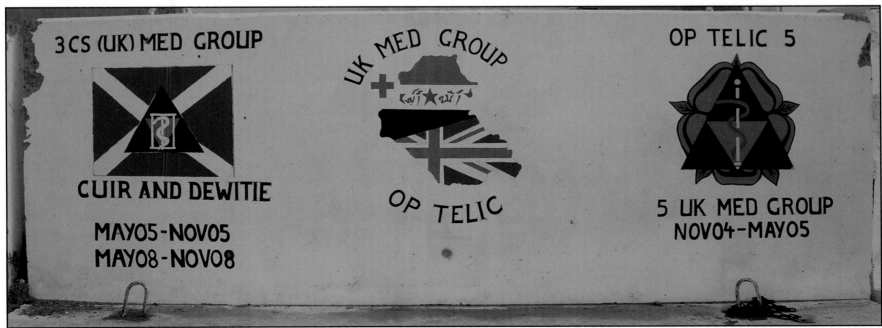

Don't weep for me
O' Land of the free
When it was my time to fall
'Twas for my country's call
'Twas for the land that I loved
That I gave my all
And for the land that I loved
I did freely give
And in her freedom
And her courage
I'll continue to live

MEMORIAL WALLS

TUSKEGEE AIRMEN-407 AEG   49
CAMP ADDER MEMORIAL   88

MAJOR STUART M. ANDERSON
SGT DANIEL J. BEARD
FRED BRYANT
PFC TROY COOPER
SGT JESSICA CAWVEY
SGT GERMAINE DEBRO
SPC DARYL DENT

CW2 BARRY EDWARDS
SPC RAYMOND J FAULSTICH
VERNON GASTON
SPC GREGORY GOODRICH
PFC ISAIAH HUNT
SPC KENNETH HAINES
DUSTIN JACKSON
DR. MARTIN LUTHER KING
SGT ELMER KRAUSE
SPC CHARLES LAMB

SPC VINCENT MADURO
PV 2 BARRY MAYO
SGT SHAWNA MORRISON
SGT JOSEPH NURRE
SGT IVORY PHIPPS
SGT ROCKY PAYNE
SPC JEREMY RIDLEN
SGT ERICH SMALLWOOD
SGT BRAD WENTZ

SPC GREGORY GOODRICH
SGT ELMER KRAUSE

SGT GERMAINE DEBRO

VERNON GASTON - Lampasas, TX

FRED BRYANT - Jacksonville, FL

PFC ISAIAH HUNT - Green Bay, WI
497TH TRANS. CO. - FT. LEWIS, WA

SGT ROCKY PAYNE - Howell, UT
497TH TRANS. CO. - FT. LEWIS, WA

SPC JEREMY RIDLEN - Moroa, IL
1544TH TRANS. CO. - IL ARMY N.G.

SPC CHARLES LAMB - Martinsville, IL
1544TH TRANS. CO. - IL ARMY N.G.

SGT SHAWNA MORRISON - Paris, IL
1544TH TRANS. CO. - IL ARMY N.G.

SGT JESSICA CAWVEY - Normal, IL
1544TH TRANS. CO. - IL ARMY N.G.

SPC DARYL DENT - Washington, DC
547TH TRANS. CO. - DC ARMY N.G.

MAJ Stuart M. Anderson

7 January 2006

Served-Operation Iraqi Freedom
I & IV

"Always Our
Dog Wonder!"

"I have a dream..."

What ... dream?

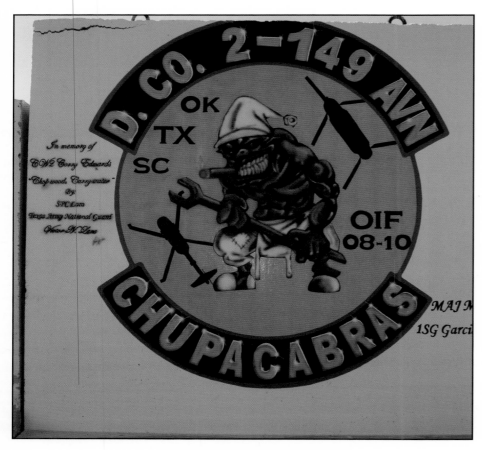

CW2 BARRY EDWARDS

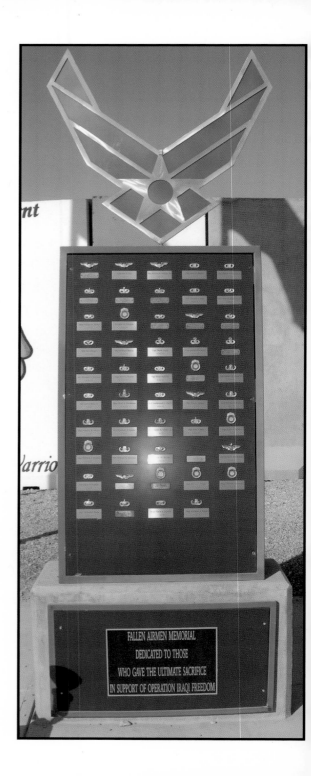

407 AEG

PHIPPS TROOP
MEDICAL CLINIC

'I will maintain the
utmost respect for
human life"
-Declaration of Geneva

4145

Dedicated to
SGT Ivory Phipps
and to all who have made
the ultimate sacrifice

DUSTIN JACKSON

SGT DANIEL J. BEARD

SPC KENNETH HAINES
SPC VINCENT MADURO
PFC TROY COOPER
PV2 BARRY MAYO

SGT BRAD A. WENTZ

SGT ERICH SMALLWOOD

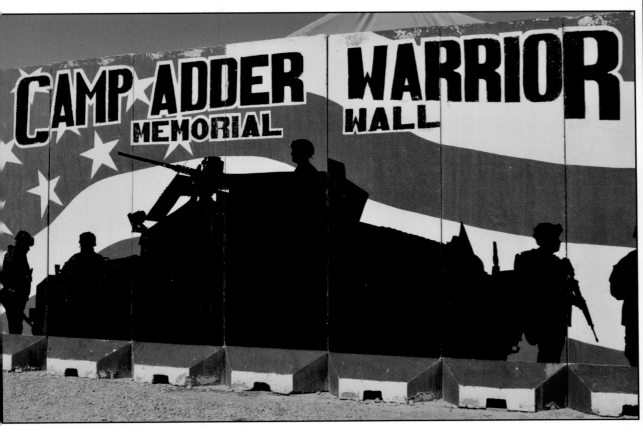

CAMP ADDER MEMORIAL WALL
(visable names)

SPC   JAMAAL R. ADDISON
CPT   TRISTAN N. AITKEN
SPC   DANIEL J. BEARD
SSG   WILLIAM J. BEARDSLEY
PFC   WILFRED BELLARD
2LT   MANCU V. BOGDAN
SPC   MATTHEW G. BOULE
SSG   JUANTREA T. BRADLEY
SPC   LARRY K. BROWN
SGT   JACOB L. BUTLER
SGT   JAMES D. CARROLL
SSG   THOMAS W. CLEMONS
SPC   DANIEL F. J. CUNNINGHAM
CPL   MICHAEL E CURTAIN
SPC   DARYL DAVIS
SSG   SEAN D. DIAMOND

SPC   PHILIP A. DODSON, JR
PVT   RUBEN ESTRELLA-SOTO
SGT   JOSHUA A. FORD
SPC   MARCUS S. FUTRELL
PFC   LEONARD J. GULCZYNSKI
CWO   ERIK A. HALVERSON
SGT   KYLE J. HARRINGTON
SSG   JEFFREY HOLMES
2LT   GROSARU IOAN
SPC   DUSTIN C. JACKSON
CWO   SCOTT JAMAR
PVT   DEVON D. JONES
2LT   JEFFREY J. KAYLOR
SSG   DALE J. KELLY
SPC   JAMES M. KIEHL
SGT   BRENT W. KOCH

CPT   EDWARD J. KORN
SSG   NINO D. LIVAUDIS
SPC   RYAN P. LONG
SGT   DERRICK K. LUTTERS
CWO   JOHNNY Y. MATA
PFC   JASON M. MEYER
PFC   ANTHONY S. MILLER
SPC   GEORGE MITCHELL
SGT   MICHAEL F. PEDERSON
PFC   LORI ANN PIESTEWA
PVT   KELLEY S. PREWITT
SPC   BRANDON RAMSEY
SGT   TODD J. ROBBINS
SPC   BRANDON J. ROWE
SGT   JOSHUA A. SCHMIDT
SGT   JASON A. SCHUMANN

SPC   BENJAMIN J. SLAVIN
CWO   ERIC A. SMITH
SFC   PAUL R. SMITH
SGT   RODERIC A. SOLOMON
SSG   ROBERT A. STEVER
SPC   CARLA J. STEWART
SPC   BRANDON S. TOBLER
SGT   PHILIP L. TRAVIS
SSG   DAVID M. VEYERKA
SFC   MIRASAK VIDHYARKORN
SGT   BRANDON L. WALLACE
SGT   DONALD R. WALTERS
PFC   MICHAEL R.C. WELDON
SGT   EUGENE WILLIAMS
SFC   ANTHONY L. WOODHAM